Reclaiming The American Dream

The Keys To Financial Freedom

Bill Quain, Ph.D.

Second Edition

Printed in the United States of America
November 1994
Second Edition

ISBN 0-9623646-1-4

Published by Wales Publishing Company

Table of Contents

Acknowledgements and Dedication

This book would not have been possible without the help of many fine professionals. My special thanks to the following people for their assistance with editing, writing and manuscript preparation:

Laura Klee, Ed Suchora, Ed Wolpert, Michael Thomas, Jeanna Knowles, my wife Jeanne Quain, and my mother, Kay Quain

Many thanks to Bill Ryan of Wales Publishing Company for producing the book.

This book is dedicated to Ron and Sharon

"The students have become the teachers"

v

Note From the Author

The subtitle to this book, *The Keys To Financial Freedom,* is based on an important principle. Like most people, you are probably very busy. So, I have selected the most important concepts of this book and marked them with *Keys*.

 Look for this symbol throughout the book. Whenever you see a picture of a key, you will know that you have reached an important point.

That's the principle of this book - to quickly give you *The Keys To Financial Freedom.*

Introduction

"What is the highest salary I can expect from a job?"

The question came from a young woman who was seated in my office at the university where I teach in the business school.

She was serious.

I was appalled.

She was a 21 year old, smart, responsible, energetic and popular individual, with excellent leadership potential. Yet she wanted to know what someone else would allow her to earn.

 She wanted me, and her future employer, to tell her what she could expect the limits of her own potential would be! Where had we gone wrong?

She is typical of the majority of people. She is one of us.

I found myself thinking, "What can people do to break the bonds that limit our ability to create wealth? What can I tell these students about opportunity, freedom, and self determination?"

My Life - My Choices

When I was 21, I didn't know much, but I did know that working for someone else was not for me. By that time, I had already successfully owned and operated two businesses. At the age of 19, I had a hotel in a resort area. By the next year, my partner and I ran a small restaurant as well. It was hard work, but the rewards were equal to the effort.

I discovered, very early in life, that this country offered each person a great gift. The gift is FREE ENTERPRISE. Anyone, I mean anyone, can own their own business, set their own goals and achieve whatever they want - without limits!

What a revelation!

My friends made different choices. They took jobs and were told how much they would make.

It didn't matter how hard they worked, they would still be paid the same hourly rate. Many of them are still facing limits to their earning potential. Although now, it's even more restrictive. Now they are on salaries. So, even if they work more hours, they still make the same amount.

And who determines the amount they make? It doesn't matter, because if *someone else* determines their salary, their potential, then they will always be under rewarded.

Throughout my life, I have tried to make choices that would not limit my potential. Yes, I am a full time professor, but I also am a speaker, writer and small business owner. I always want to be in a position that allows me the freedom to reach the greatest potential for which I am capable.

The only way to do that is to participate in the free enterprise opportunities of business ownership.

A Long Search

Even though I wanted no part of a system that meant virtual slavery to bosses, restrictive policies and salary caps, I had not found a solution that could be offered to others. After all, traditional business ownership requires vast start up capital, overwhelming government interference and the costs of inventory, employees and buildings. And, there is the issue of time.

Who has the capital and time to invest in their own business? Certainly my students did not. Neither did most of the participants in the training sessions and seminars I provided.

Yet, I knew that people were becoming wealthy. I could see it. Where did they get their money? How did they achieve their lifestyles?

I decided to find out. I owed it to my students, my friends and myself. I began in the "normal" places, looking at the corporate and professional worlds. The answer wasn't there.

Finally, I found it. A system that was so simple, yet vastly effective, that the potential was literally unlimited. I knew I had to study it, to examine it. If it met the claims of those who were already making a fantastic living in this system, I knew I would write a book about it. Obviously, this system has made it!

Take My Advice - Or Not!

After carefully reviewing, analyzing and observing this system, I am able to recommend it to anyone with a desire to attain financial freedom. It is foolproof!

But, everyone must make their own decisions. While the business does not require money, it does demand self control, commitment and motivation.

You will find the answers to four questions in this book:

1. Why do you need a free enterprise based business of your own?

2. What is this business?

3. What will you be doing?

4. Will it work for you?

So What Do I Tell My Students?

Remember the young lady that I mentioned at the beginning of this book? What should I tell her, and others like her?

Now I tell them that there are alternatives. They do not have to resign themselves to a life of salary caps, downsizing and layoffs. I can tell them that free enterprise is alive and well.

My advice to them, and to you, is to dare to be different. Look for possibilities, not restraints. Find a reliable system with a proven track record. Make the most of opportunities by examining each one with an open mind. Use the free enterprise system and live life as an entrepreneur. In short, RECLAIM THE AMERICAN DREAM!

Part One:
Why Are Americans Looking?

CHAPTER ONE
WHAT'S IN IT FOR ME?

You have just received a book that may change your life.

This book is designed to awaken you to a system that is proving to be the most significant economic transition of this generation.

You're probably asking yourself, "What's in it for me?"

Let me tell you.

Any ambitious individual now has the opportunity for increased wealth and personal growth.

Freedom And Choice

Few people wholeheartedly believe they can be totally financially free. Free from debt, financial worry and control by others. Imagine the feeling!

It is the American Dream, but most consider it out of reach today. Nothing could be further from the truth.

What would it mean to you? What would it mean for your family? Absolute freedom to pursue the things that are most important to you.

Being free means having choices - choosing to do whatever you want, to go to work or not, to allow a spouse to stay home to take care of the family.

What about vacations? Many people say "We can't travel, we have small children". What they are really saying is "We don't have the money and time to travel with the children". If you have enough money, you can bring along a baby sitter. You can rent an extra hotel room, or a suite of rooms. The kids would really enjoy their time with you, and when you needed it, you could enjoy some time away from the kids.

You see? Choices are part of freedom. Do you have all the freedom and choices that you need?

A System And A Mentor

A mentor is a teacher. A mentor is a person that you respect, one who has already been successful. We have all had such role models in our lives, people who we respected and admired. We saw something in them that we wanted to see in ourselves. We did what they did, so we would have what they had. Imagine if you could find a *system* and a *large, unlimited supply of mentors* to help make you wealthy.

 Imagine, successful entrepreneurs acting as MENTORS and showing others how to use a SYSTEM - mentors that want you to succeed. Its a win-win situation.

As you grow, you will become a mentor to others. You will help them to succeed. How will that affect you?

You will experience astonishing personal growth. You will become a better listener and a greater leader. You will develop great friendships. You will become wealthy.

That's what's in it for you.

Who Will Pay My Bills?

With the huge corporate cloud casting a shadow on the economic environment, most people are unable to grasp the total concept of reaching their dreams. They are too worried about tomorrow. The enormity of the current recession has taken a serious toll on millions.

Being short of cash is certainly not a recent trend. There always seems to be more month than money. Maybe you would simply like to pay off some bills and "get out from under it or break even". Well, the opportunity and system are now in place.

If you only want a few hundred dollars a month to help with a mortgage payment; you can do that. If you want to start saving for your children's education, you can do that. If you are sick and tired of being sick and tired, you can change that right now.

All you need is commitment. There are systems and mentors creating the solution at this moment.

A Lifelong Income - And Beyond

The entrepreneurial business opportunity with a win-win scenario, developed over the past 30 years, offers residual income. That's vastly different than income from wages.

 A residual income provides you and your heirs with a steady, dependable cash flow, even if you are unable to work. It's better than having money in the bank, and living off the interest.

This is possible because of a relatively new type of business. It is a business that rewards people for their work. It provides profit sharing and incentives. It is the best part of the free enterprise system. You will own your own business, without the dangers inherent in most businesses. You will be inspired, motivated and helped, with little overhead and/or capital.

 It will not happen overnight. It will take a few years of dedicated work. However, at the end of that time, total freedom is the reward.

Wealth By Association

Look around you. Are you surrounding yourself with positive influences? Are you a positive influence on others?

The only way to succeed, and I mean the ONLY way, is to live a positive life, surrounded by positive, successful people.

It's simple. You can choose to be "one of the gang" and remain a prisoner, a slave of the bosses who control your life. Or, you can look for the people who have already made it.

What's in it for you? You will become like the people you admire. They will teach you. You will teach others. You will be an active, intelligent contributor to your own fortune.

What Is WEALTH?

Each person must determine what wealth means to them. It may simply be to break even each month. It may be much more.

Wealth is freedom. Wealth is personal development. It is the opportunity to share, give and receive. Family, friends and lifestyle are all part of the total picture.

You can have wealth. You can grow, prosper and achieve. Entrepreneurship can provide you with economic rewards, recognition, status, fulfillment and love.

You can learn to love yourself by helping others to achieve. True success will be built on the success of others through sharing a commitment to worthwhile ideals. Increasing or unlimited commitment, recognition, time, love and financial rewards; that's wealth.

That's what's in it for you. That's why the win-win mentor system of entrepreneurship is overcoming the traditionally structured hierarchial system of the less effective Corporate Kingdom. The keys to wealth are waiting for you. Each of us must apply the ingredients of enthusiasm, determination and belief in our abilities, or we will not have the energy to overcome the obstacles, and set ourselves totally free.

CHAPTER TWO
A BUSINESS REVOLUTION:
A RETURN TO OWNERSHIP

This chapter briefly traces the development of business trends in America. We will examine the cycle of business ownership and entrepreneurial free enterprise. You will see how the American economy - built on the principles of free enterprise - is once again offering individuals an outstanding opportunity to take charge of their lives, secure their financial futures, and live as free men and women.

The economic forces that shape our daily lives are changing rapidly due to the massive improvements and innovations in new technology. Our world is shrinking as we become exposed to the ideas, dreams, hopes and innovations offered by people from around the globe. But, few Americans have utilized the economic opportunities offered by globalization to improve their own lives.

Each individual must prepare themselves to face the challenges and seize the opportunities offered by the swiftly changing technological and economic situation.

Free Enterprise In America

The U.S. economy was originally based on a concept of entrepreneurs working together to create free enterprise and free capitalism. The merchant class (the entrepreneurs of the day), was the backbone of the American revolution. These individuals were unwilling to bear the tyranny of a system that placed class structure and government interference above the dreams of the individual. The American economy was founded on the principle that each person had the right to pursue their own financial dreams.

The founders of the United States had very strong economic as well as political views. Their economic values were best reflected by the writings of Adam Smith, a noted economist of the day. His powerful economic credo, defined in his epic work *The Wealth of Nations,* declared that all men should be allowed to seek the benefits of free enterprise through their own hard work.

The Rise Of The Entrepreneur

Business flourished in post revolutionary America, built upon the individual. Inventors brought great innovations to the marketplace. American entrepreneurs seized these technologies and put them to work.

As immigrants swarmed to American shores, they carried with them a dream - to own a business of their own, to have land, and to secure a place for their family. Most of all, they saw opportunity.

They did not fear work. They only feared a lack of opportunity.

The Industrial Revolution

The Industrial Revolution was a time of vast economic and social change. Great factories sprang up using the new technologies. Workers were needed to produce the standardized goods that were now so popular. The great waves of immigrants were funneled into foundries, factories and plants. The American Dream turned from self ownership to full employment.

It is this legacy of trading time for money that is such a strong part of our system today. Unfortunately, it is also one of the primary causes for the weakening of our social fabric.

Of course the industrial revolution did spur a continued increase in the standard of living. Machines and new technologies made life easier. But it was the leaders of the industrial revolution, not the great numbers of workers, who grew wealthy. These entrepreneurs learned to combine the work of many people with improving technology to reap outstanding incomes.

One of the major reasons that the industrial revolution was so prominent and successful is that it reduced costs. According to economist Paul Zane Pilzer, at the time of the industrial revolution, the cost of goods that appeared on the store shelf was 85% for manufacture and 15% for distribution. Any new technology that could reduce manufacturing costs led to huge profits. The leading entrepreneurs of the industrial revolution were the

technicians who were able to reduce this cost.   Henry
Ford was a prime example.

Today, cost structures are vastly different.
Only 15% of the cost of most goods are
attributable to manufacturing. 85% of the
costs of goods on retail shelves are distribution. This is
an important premise for the entrepreneurs of today
who wish to seize opportunities.

Post World War II

The mobilization of the American industrial complex
helped the U.S. emerge from the war as the leading
economic world power. While the rest of the world was
rebuilding from the carnage, U.S. factories were in full
production. Returning servicemen were eager to reclaim
their jobs and forge a new future.   They wanted the
sacrifices they made to become the foundation for a new
land - bright with the American Dream.

And the post war years seemed to have it all.   The
American Dream had now firmly shifted from business
ownership to a new model. Veterans used the G.I. Bill
to attend college in record numbers.   Men who had
learned to fight and win a war by working in the rigid
military structure were now applying that same theory to
their corporate structures.

The American Dream could now be summed as: "Get a
good education, get a good job, save money, buy a
home, retire and be happy". For the next two and a half
decades, this was a plausible dream.

The Rise Of The Corporation

Huge corporations became the most significant and visible sign of economic security. Layer upon layer of workers, supervisors, middle managers and executives were formed. A man or woman could work their whole lives for a single corporate giant.

New technologies were again creating opportunities for corporations. The massive amounts of capital needed to enter new markets precluded individuals from gaining power. The cost of distribution was staggering. It required a huge conglomerate to produce goods, then put them into the hands of the consumer.

The structures created in this era became the "Corporate Kingdom." The heads of the kingdom, the corporate royals, ruled with almost limitless power. They were able to do this for two simple reasons: they could move goods from the factory to the consumer, and they had the only access to information.

The Problem with the Corporate Kingdom

There were outstanding factors that contributed to corporate America's downfall, one of which was an inability to react to global competition.

Consider the automobile industry. American cars have improved greatly in quality - but only because the Japanese were stealing the market by creating exceptional service and dependability. It took American industry many years to catch on. Now, much of the damage has been done. Hundreds of thousands of Americans have lost their jobs. And they will never get them back!

A second problem, the lack of incentives, is perhaps even more devastating. The structure of the Corporate Kingdom has almost eliminated the motivation of the average worker and executive to create improved service and quality. The reason is very simple.

You will almost never be allowed to make all the money that you want.

 Think about it. Has anyone ever sat down and asked you what you want? Has anyone ever said "We are concerned about you. We want to make sure that you can make all the money you need to reach your dreams."? Probably not.

Remember this: if you want to create security, wealth and financial freedom, it will never happen if you work for someone else.

Global Competition

Global competition is a direct result of the technologies that have made it possible to cross borders electronically. Even relatively poor countries can now acquire the technology necessary to compete on a world wide basis. And this trend directly affects the job security of Americans.

In response to the influx of global competitors, American members of the Corporate Kingdom have begun to create leaner, meaner corporate staffs. This means corporate downsizing - layoffs.

That's right, global competition, a term that most people didn't pay much attention to, is directly impacting YOUR security.   You could be laid off so that your corporation can compete with the world's citizens!

Everyone knows somebody who has been laid off or forced to retire early. Perhaps you have been laid off yourself. Most people blame it on the recession of the early 90's. But if it was the recession, those jobs would come back as soon as the downturn was over. Do you think those jobs are coming back? I don't.

Here is a list of some of the jobs lost from American corporations in the last few years. Did you work for one of these companies? If you were not laid off, do you really believe that you have security in your job? When will your company downsize?

Company	Staff Cutbacks
IBM	85,000
AT&T	83,500
General Motors	74,000
U.S. Postal Service	55,000
Sears	50,000
Boeing	30,000
NYNEX	22,000
Hughes Aircraft	21,000
GTE	17,000
Martin-Marietta	15,000
DuPont	14,800
Eastman Kodak	14,000
Philip Morris	14,000
Procter & Gamble	13,000
Phar Mor	13,000
Bank Of America	12,000
Aetna	11,800
GE Aircraft Engines	10,250
McDonnell Douglas	10,200
BellSouth	10,200
Ford Motor	10,000
Xerox	10,000
Pacific Telesis	10,000
Honeywell	9,000
U.S. West	9,000

*reprinted from _Business Week_, May 9, 1994.

Globalization And You

The average person does not picture themselves as a global force. Yet, according to author John Naisbitt, the individual *is* at the center of power. This is due to the Global Paradox. The Global Paradox is this - "While the changes in technology now offer large corporations the ability to compete globally, these same advances give individuals tremendous power - the power of information and networking".

Globalization has only been possible through communications technology. This technology is available inexpensively to almost anyone.

Richard Poe, author of *Wave Three*, agrees with Naisbitt. Both of them point out the value of computers, voice mail, fax machines, networks, etc.

For a very small investment, individual entrepreneurs can develop a home based office that can tap into the communications power of a world wide network. This is the trend that can set you free financially!

Over 200 years ago, Adam Smith predicted that entrepreneurs would work together in networks to create a powerful free enterprise system. He could not have imagined the technological revolution. However, his basic idea is alive - and thriving - today.

You do not have to be a computer whiz to take advantage of the new opportunities. In fact, you do not even need to own or operate any of this equipment. You only need to be willing to work hard and to associate yourself with entrepreneurs who have already put this technology network into action.

Franchising

Franchises take advantage of communications technology and focus on standardization. They began to develop in earnest in the 1970's. Today, they are a familiar fixture on the business scene.

Franchises offer several advantages. First, they reduce risk. By following a system, entrepreneurs can increase their chances for business survival. Once a system has been developed, it can be taught to others.

A franchise is, in fact, a network of professionals. Adam Smith would surely approve of franchises.

Franchises also offer individual ownership. The franchisees have virtually no limits to their income. If they work hard, follow the system and stay with the program, they can become wealthy.

On the other hand, there are several distinct disadvantages to franchising. The monetary investment can be huge. It requires almost $1 million to open a McDonalds franchise. Buildings, inventory, maintenance, etc, require large amounts of capital.

Most franchises require the operation of a traditional business. The franchisee must hire managers or be present during all operating hours. And, the number of employees needed to run a successful, traditional business can be a real headache. They may be unmotivated, unwilling and unable to do a good job.

A franchisor once told me "Many people just end up *buying a job rather than owning a business"*. Instead of buying freedom, they simply buy another grueling place of employment.

 But what if there was a system that had the advantages of franchising - business ownership, professional networking and assistance, without the disadvantages? Wouldn't that be terrific? Imagine, limitless potential with no inventory, no employees and no capital requirements.

The Greatest Business Opportunity In Your Lifetime

Where will you be five years from now? Will you still be watching the world go by?

 The question is, "Will you believe your own instincts?" You know that your financial future is at risk. Now, all you have to do is take advantage of the economic opportunities and GO!

Consider these two important facts:

1.   Distribution - bringing goods and services from the producers to the consumers - represents <u>85%</u> of the costs of doing business.

2.   Technology has made it possible for individuals - I mean ordinary people - to work together to take advantage of the changing economy - and to make fortunes.

If you could use a network of entrepreneurs to tap into the riches offered by reducing distribution costs, would you be interested? And if the money it took to get involved was only a few hundred dollars, would that sweeten the offer? If you were given assistance by other people who had already become rich, free and independent, would that make it even more interesting? I think it would!

Enter Networking

In the 1950's, when franchising was in its infancy, another financial movement began to take hold. It was developed to bring consumers and producers together - reducing distribution costs.

Network marketing was similar to Adam Smith's concept of free enterprise, with several improvements. Unlike the Corporate Kingdom, network marketing has limitless potential for individuals. Unlike franchising, the entry costs are low, and most distributors have neither inventory nor employees. And with the technological revolution, network marketers can be "plugged into" a system that makes managing their business easy and efficient.

Many large corporations have now seen the benefits of direct distribution and are creating network companies of their own. Proctor and Gamble, Campbell's, Gillete, and other big names are already seizing the opportunity. Other companies are utilizing existing networks to help increase distribution efficiency.

You are now in a position to gain financial freedom by simply joining the most profound business change that has occurred in America. Millions of people are reclaiming their birth right and securing their financial freedom. Join them!

CHAPTER THREE
NO LOYALTY FROM ROYALTY

Almost 90% of the working population works for a corporation of some kind. Bankers, carpenters, salespeople, middle managers and top executives report to these institutions. Even physicians and attorneys have corporate bosses. It is the traditional business entity that <u>rules</u> our working lives.

And "**RULES**" is the operative word!

While corporations do create jobs and provide income for hundreds of thousands, their appeal has begun to diminish. The Corporate Kingdom is asleep when it comes to rewarding its participants with the real potential of economic freedom.

The alarm has been sounded. The Corporate Kingdom has serious shortcomings that can make it impossible for you to reach your financial goals and dreams.

There are five major failures within the Corporate Kingdom.
1. Corporate royalty
2. Internal competition
3. Killing incentives
4. Resisting change
5. Denying ownership

1. THE CORPORATE ROYALTY

Who are the corporate royals? They are the top managers immune from the consequences of the bad decisions they may make every day. They are the ones with the "Let them eat cake" attitude towards the people who actually do the hard work in the organizations.

Harpers Magazine, 9/93, reports that the average CEO of a large U.S. corporation earns $3.8 million/year.

Here is the most amazing part. Who decides salaries and benefits of the CEO? In most corporations it is the Board of Directors. _And who appoints the Board of Directors?_

You guessed it, the CEO. So the kings have their courts.

 How do these corporate royals operate their kingdoms? By controlling information, setting rules, holding power, and utilizing the force of fear.

2. INTERNAL COMPETITION

There is a story about two hikers that exemplifies the attitude found in the Corporate Kingdom:

Bill and Joe were on a hike in the deep woods. Suddenly, on the path ahead of them, a huge bear reared up and began to claw the air, growling fiercely. The bear dropped to all fours and started running down the path, directly towards the two hikers.

Joe thought quickly and took action. He reached into his backpack and removed a pair of running shoes. Quickly, he sat down on the ground, took off his hiking boots, and put on his running shoes.

Bill saw what was going on and exclaimed "Joe, what are you doing? You can't out run a bear!"

"I don't have to out run a bear" said Joe, "I only have to out run YOU!"

That is the attitude of most career minded corporate officers or employees. You don't have to be the best to succeed, you only have to be better than the people you work with.

Wouldn't it be great if our success depended on the success of others? What if a system existed where instead of trying to achieve personal success, we helped others to succeed? And in turn, we were rewarded because we made them successful.

3. KILLING INCENTIVES

The Corporate Kingdom is killing incentives. Where is the motivation to succeed? The deck is stacked. The fight is fixed. The jury is rigged.

What motivates people on the job? What gives them the incentive to work? Most of us work out of necessity.

Yes, some people really love their jobs. But would you continue to work if they did not give you a paycheck?

Many companies do have recognition programs. However, is it enough to be named "Employee of the Month" if at the end of that month you still do not have enough money to pay your bills?

Consider this: you are paid the least amount of money that it would take to replace you.

If they could find someone else to do the job as well as you do it, at a lower rate of pay, many companies would jump at the chance.

Consider this appalling fact. In the Corporate Kingdom, you cannot make any more than your boss makes! So if he or she is underpaid, you will be too!

Take the case of Janet (not her real name, but a true story). She was a salesperson for a health care facility. Her job was to sell wellness programs and other health care services to corporations. Her company had never had someone in this position before, but increased competition from other facilities made it necessary to reach out to the customers.

Janet was hired because she had a track record of success with another company. She was given a pay package that had a reasonable base salary and a commission on her sales.

Janet did a superb job and started making sale after sale. Her commission began to really add up. She was making a great deal of money, and so was the facility.

The trouble was, Janet's bosses were not making a lot of money. The facility's profits didn't help either of them. They didn't receive a bonus when the facility made more money.

So what did the corporation do? They reduced Janet's commissions so she wouldn't make as much.

Their reasoning: "We didn't know you would make so many sales," they said.

Without knowing it, Janet had committed the greatest sin in the Corporate Kingdom. She had made more money than her bosses. And the antiquated system cannot tolerate that.

4. RESISTING CHANGE

Resistance to change is not a phenomena that is strictly limited to the Corporate Kingdom. Most people hate to change. Yet, the future will force you to change, and your survival depends on it.

The Corporate Kingdom is still living in the 1950's. At that time, families were together as a general rule. The man went to work and the woman stayed home with the children. Most people could live on one income and still achieve their financial dreams.

Of course, times have changed, but the Corporate Kingdom still sells the myth that if you work and are loyal to the company, you will be successful.

Try to convince the family with both parents in the corporate work force, day care responsibilities, a big mortgage and a mountain of debt that they have reached their financial dreams. It just isn't so.

Despite the obvious changes in the needs of employees, the Corporate Kingdom has slept through the uproar.

The typical employee is a member of a two worker family - or a single parent. However, corporate policies and practices simply pretend that this is not so.

In the United States today, 60% of mothers with young children are full time employees. Yet, most companies do not give them time off when their children are sick.

Employees must deal with having children in day care and spending time away from families, without ever really achieving their financial goals. Times have changed, but for the most part, corporations have not.

5. DENYING OWNERSHIP

In "How to be Rich," billionaire industrialist J. Paul Getty said the first condition for financial success is to own your own business.

What does ownership do? Ownership puts you in charge, master of your own destiny. Your hard work is directly rewarded with profit. You make the decisions and reap the rewards.

J. Paul Getty had it right - you need to work for yourself.

To be really successful, risk is necessary. The trick, however, is to minimize the risk and maximize the potential for making money.

Personal business ownership is a remarkable stimulus for motivation. Consider the immigrant family that operates their own business. Motivational speaker Zig Ziglar recently stated that immigrants have a four times greater chance to become millionaires than do people who are born in the United States. Part of the reason may be that many own their own businesses.

Corporations have failed to provide ownership for their employees, and this leads to a terrible situation. Workers simply "put in time" at work. They know that additional work or better performance will not result in long term economic fitness. All they have to do is stay out of trouble and hope that they do not get laid off. Their rewards will not be any more or any less.

A FINAL WORD

The Corporate Kingdom exists, and you probably work within it. You don't need anyone to tell you that it will not meet your financial needs for the future. It probably isn't meeting them right now.

Over the years, a bureaucratic system of doing business has evolved, and now must change, or fail.

The lure of the corporate myth is strong and almost overpowering. We are told that if we work hard, we will have the American Dream - own a home, take vacations, send our children to good schools, etc. But it simply has not proven to be true.

The myth is over. If you depend on the Corporate Kingdom for financial success you will surely be disappointed.

Government And Education - No Help There!

Governments do not reward people for hard work and initiative. That is a fact demonstrated by the social welfare and averaging programs that are laid at our feet for the taking.

The More You Make, The Less You Keep

In his audio tape "Economic Paradigms," economist Paul Zane Pilzer describes the rationale for a progressive income tax. (Progressive income tax means that you are taxed at a higher rate, or percentage, when you make more money.)

He relates how in the 1930's President Franklin Roosevelt initiated this tax system.

The theory of the day was that every American would soon have a four bedroom house and a car. At that point, economists claimed, people would all stop working.

Why would they stop working? Because they had all achieved their dreams. So, a tax was instituted with increasingly higher percentages. The idea was that people would never fully achieve their dreams, and would therefore continue to work.

Brilliant! Right?

Wrong!

Yet, the theory was widely adopted and, eventually, the highest tax bracket was about 90%. When Ronald Reagan took office, the highest bracket was still 70%. It was greatly reduced during subsequent administrations, but it is slowly climbing back up. (Maybe not so slowly.)

IMITATION IVORY: THE IVORY TOWER

We hear a lot of stories about students who graduate from high school, and even college, and are not able to read or write properly. The newspapers and television journalists are always crying about some high school class that couldn't find the United States on a map of the world. And, of course, we are falling behind the rest of the industrialized nations in test scores on math and science.

But, these are not the real problems with our educational system.

 We are teaching our children to function in a system that will no longer meet their needs in the future!

A study in Fortune magazine, 1/93, showed some startling statistics.

> If a 38 year old couple earns $85,000 per year in 1993 and they wish to retire at age 60 and maintain their lifestyle, they will need a retirement fund of $4.6 MILLION!

Where in our educational system do we teach our children this?

When I first saw this figure, I didn't believe it. However, it is true.

Then I thought "Why didn't someone tell me this?" I surprised myself with my honest answer.

I am a professor in a College of Business Administration. If I wasn't telling people this, who would?

You see, we are educating our children to become "cogs in the wheel," rather than leaders and thinkers. We are not providing them with the information that they need to make intelligent decisions about their futures.

Who Are The Teachers?

We are taught by our parents, teachers, professors and peers (not to mention television).

And, what are they teaching us?

Our parents and teachers gave us a simple message: study in school, work hard, pay taxes and obey the law. If we did those things, we would be successful, we would have the American Dream.

Our peers taught us to stay in the group. Be a team player. The problem is, the team wasn't going anywhere either. If we started to do things that the group was not doing, they slowly reeled us in.

Our teachers could not teach us to look outside the system, because they were all part of the system.

Think about it. What did you learn in school? You learned to add, write sentences and memorize formulas.

Did anyone ever ask you to challenge the system?

Copernicus challenged the system. He discovered that the earth and other planets rotate around the sun.

Columbus challenged the system. He discovered a new world.

Steve Jobs challenged the system. Working in his garage, he put unlimited creativity and communication abilities in the hands of millions of ordinary people by developing Apple computers.

Rich De Vos and Jay Van Andel challenged the system. They developed a marketing system that enabled millions of hard working people to attain financial freedom through network marketing, a multilevel marketing profit sharing structure.

In fact, it is only when we look outside the currently accepted methods of thinking that we make great strides and discover the potential in ourselves.

But we don't let successful people teach us. Many people are content to sit in front of the television, watching other people lead their lives. We need to find successful people, learn from them and become successful ourselves.

Your life is too valuable to trust it to someone who has not succeeded in their own life.

CHAPTER FOUR
THE STATE OF THE
AMERICAN DREAM:
LET'S GET PERSONAL

What is the American Dream, where did it go, and what can you do to get it back? It is not too late to reclaim the American Dream, but we must first understand what it is, and what has happened to it.

The American Dream

I am a consultant to the "Knowledge Company," which is based in Washington, D.C. It is owned by an attorney who assists people who wish to emigrate to the United States. He works strictly with professionals, people who have the equivalent of a college degree. In many cases, these professionals will make less in the United States than they did in their home countries.

I asked the attorney why people would go to so much trouble and expense to get a job for less money. His answer was surprising.

He said that people come to the U.S. for the opportunity - not the money. We have the opportunity in the U.S. to create our own freedom.

Isn't it amazing that we take this opportunity for granted, while outsiders see it as the promise of freedom?

So, the American Dream is based on opportunity. It is a starting point. We each have the opportunity to achieve financial freedom.

Trading Time For Dollars

We really began to lose the American Dream when we started trading time for money. This happens whenever you give up the idea of business ownership and take a job. There are several problems with trading time for money:

1.   You only have so much time, therefore, you can only have so much money.

2.   Instead of being your own boss, you give someone else power over your future.

3.   Due to global competition and corporate downsizing, there is no longer any security in a job.

4.   When you stop trading time for money, you stop getting money.

If you trade your time for money, you are helping someone else achieve their dreams. Your dreams, hopes and aspirations are not important.

But the most appalling part of trading time for dollars is that when you stop, so does the money.

Yet, there is absolutely no reason why you should actually have to work for the rest of your life. If you receive residual income, you continue to get income even if you are not putting in time. This is freedom!

Residual income is created by ownership. If you own your company, you receive income long after you stop working.

For right now, consider this definition of the American Dream. See if this is a better idea than trading time for dollars.

 The American Dream: Using the opportunities you have to build your own business, creating residual income, and setting yourself financially free. Making the choices you think are best for you and your family.

Retirement - How?

Have you ever heard anyone say "I can't wait to retire and live on Social Security"? Of course not. Most people figure that they will have some combination of Social Security and retirement pay. Yet, recent studies have demonstrated the absolute foolishness of this theory for most people.

In an article in *Success Magazine* (12/93), author Mark Yarnell presents an appalling set of statistics. Examine the chart below, which is reprinted from the article.

You will see the impossibility of living on a retirement income that is probably out of your reach to attain anyway.

	Annual Income	Monthly Savings at 8%	Total Assets at 5% Needed by Age 65	Equivalent Income at Age 65
If age 45 now	60,000	3,679	2,167,320	108,366
	35,000	2,146	1,264,260	63,213
	25,000	1,533	903,040	45,152
If age 35 now	60,000	1,954	2,912,700	145,635
	35,000	1,140	1,699,080	84,954
	25,000	814	1,213,620	60,681
If age 25 now	60,000	1,121	3,914,440	195,722
	35,000	654	2,283,420	114,171
	25,000	467	1,631,000	81,550

This article is aptly titled "The Greatest Motivator". And if these figures don't motivate you to take some action, then you are either already wealthy or kidding yourself.

The following paragraph is a quote from the article. Mr. Yarrell does an excellent job of explaining the dangers facing working Americans:

"If you're 35 years old today, making $60,000 a year, and you want to maintain that level of income in retirement at age 65, I've got scary news: Any retirement plan you've got now probably won't cover it. At current rates of inflation (3 percent), it will cost you $150,000 per year to maintain your way of life in the year 2023. If you get 5 percent interest, that will require a nest egg of $3 million. To build it, allowing for compounding interest and taxes along the way, you need to save $43,915.66 a year, starting now (see chart). If you're pulling down a salary of $60,000, that's probably your entire current after-tax income - or even a bit more".

The 40/50 Plan

 Under this plan, you can expect the following:

1. *Work 40 to 50 hours per week*
2. *Work 50 weeks per year*
3. *Work for 40 to 50 years*
4. *End up living on 40 to 50% of what you can't live on now!*

Does this sound familiar? It should. The majority of people who are employed in the workforce today are on this plan. Of course, you might be an exception; you might work more than 40 to 50 hours per week.

The 40/50 plan is our price for stability and dependability. The problem is, that when we place our fates in the hands of others, they will place too high a price on our security. The free men and women among us, the entrepreneurs and adventurers, will reap the rewards of freedom.

What happens when we lose our freedom of choice? For many people, that question isn't answered until they retire. Then, they find themselves in the uncomfortable position of being financially dependent on families or the government.

A 1989 study by the U. S. Department of Health, Education and Welfare found that for people just starting their careers, the following will exist by the time they reach the age 65:

- 29% will be dead

- 13% will have incomes under $5,200

- 55% will have incomes less than $33,000, with a median income of only $7,300

- _Only 3% will have incomes over $33,000_

This will severely limit your choices!

Planning For The Future

At a recent presentation a successful business executive quoted James B. Kidd's predictions for future retirees:

- 95% of all Americans who reach age 65 will not be able to afford the luxury of financial independence

- 22% will need to continue working

- 38% will depend entirely on public charity such as Welfare and Social Security

- 45% will be dependent on their relatives

- Only 5% will have enough money to meet their financial needs

 Only 1% of retirees will have the financial independence and DIGNITY that retirement should hold.

What kind of life is that? Imagine, we work 40 to 50 years and have nothing to show for it! And this is not a "what if" proposition. This is happening right now and will happen to you. Unless you do something about it!

The New Realities

In an article entitled,"How To Protect Your Financial Future," *Fortune Magazine*, 1/93, the author discusses four *New Realities* that apply to most of us today. We will not have to wait until retirement to experience these forces.

1.   Salaries no longer keep up with inflation, so living standards decrease and saving for the future is nearly impossible.

2.   Most middle class families depend on two incomes. About 63% of married women work.

3.   For most Americans, retirement is a fading dream. Today, retirees get about four dollars back from Social Security for every dollar they put in. When the Baby Boomers retire, it will be about one dollar for every dollar contributed.

4.   Homeowners can no longer depend on the appreciation of their homes.

A Lost Generation

There are many other signs that the American Dream is in peril. Chief among these is the plight of Generation X. This is the twenty-something group.

 For the first time in our history, the current generation will have a lower standard of living than their parents.

According to "What Happened To The American Dream", *Business Week* (8/19/91), these young people are the victims of global competition and declining productivity.

This generation has seen average salaries fall by nearly 19.8% per FAMILY. This has happened despite the fact that the majority of families now have two incomes. The results have seriously impacted the opportunities, and hence the Dream, for this group. Consider this:

- Home ownership has not only been postponed, it has dropped dramatically.

- Many young adults are forced to live with their parents.

- Unemployment is higher, and those who do work are more likely to have part time jobs.

- Their children are more likely to live below the poverty line.

- It is the first generation to live without hope of reaching their parents' lifestyle.

But the woes that have beset Generation X are not limited to those in their twenties. Many parents had not planned on their adult children living with them. This impacts the lifestyle and choices of the parents.

 We are in a crisis. Let's face the facts together and do something about it. Don't pretend that the economic future of each of us is not in peril.

In short, there is a struggle to simply maintain the status quo. Yet, under the circumstances, the status quo is not a practical situation. We can continue to struggle along, gaining a little, losing some. Or we can decide to take advantage of the unique opportunities this situation offers.

Dreams, Dreams!

Ron's family and friends thought he had one fault. Ron was a dreamer. He wanted certain things in life. When he and Sharon decided to get married, Sharon's parents were worried that this dreamer would never be able to take care of their daughter.

Well, Ron's ability to dream has been his strongest asset. At 23, he and Sharon have created their own part-time business. They have successfully contributed to their income, and are creating a lifestyle that their friends may never obtain.

Why? Because they had a dream and acted on it.

Ron and Sharon translated their dreams into obtainable goals. They then developed a plan to reach these goals. And assumed the attitude that *nothing* was going to keep them from their goals.

What happens to our dreams? For most people, they are lost in the mad rush to keep up with the financial demands of reality.

What is reality for most people? It is a mortgage, car payment, tuition bills and a two worker family. It's hard to have dreams when you're constantly short of the money and time necessary to just <u>maintain</u> your lifestyle.

So, we shrink our dreams.

Look on the wall of a young boy's bedroom. Is there a poster of a car? What is more likely to be on the poster, a Ford Escort or a Corvette? The answer is obvious.

If you don't have a dream, I can't give one to you. A dream is something you must be brave enough to seek for yourself. Are you brave enough? Or will you allow others to dictate the limits of your hopes?

I can't give you a dream, but I can show you a vehicle for reaching your dreams.

Setting Goals

Before anything can happen, you must meet two conditions.

 First, you must believe that there is some way for ordinary people to reach their dreams.

Second, you must firmly establish specific goals.

In this book, we will outline a way for ordinary people to reach their dreams. However, that is not the purpose of this book. HOW you will reach your goals is only secondary. WHY you are trying to reach them is much more important. So let's talk about the WHY?

You should set goals because you deserve more than you have right now. I mean that sincerely. Don't settle for things just because that is the way that they are today.

Do you know what you want? What is important to you? What condition in your life would you be willing to fight to improve?

Appendix A at the back of this book contains some short exercises to help you decide what you really want and what is most important to you. Why not take some time right now to compete this exercise?

But come back quickly!

When asked what is most important to them, most people list the following:

- Family
- Health
- Recreation
- Religion
- Travel
- Security

These are all noble desires. And, of course, money cannot buy these things. But it sure can make a difference.

If leisure and recreation are important to you, then you need *time and money*. Money can buy you time. Money and the time to enjoy it mean freedom.

Money is not a guarantee of health, but stress is a major source of illness and heart attacks. And lack of money can cause major stress.

Financial security is not a condition for having a family, but the major cause of marital discord is arguments over money.

Would you like to help out at your church or synagogue? What about helping less fortunate families? Financial resources can certainly make a difference!

The Courage To Change

By now, you should realize that your lifestyle is in danger. I don't think there is any doubt about that. But what will you do about it? Will you ignore it and hope it gets better, or will you face the future with courage and conviction, faith and commitment?

There will be many times in your life when the facts will rise up to challenge your basic beliefs. After all, you have been told by parents, teachers and others that the keys to success are to work hard and to reach for the American Dream.

Well, right now, the facts are probably challenging your beliefs. And, it is time to accept the facts and make some basic changes in your life.

This takes courage. The courage to change and to start fresh. I will not suggest that you quit your job. You will need the security of a paycheck while you build your financial freedom.

I will, however, ask you to change. To set goals and to work with people who have been successful.

Get Help From The Experts

When you are sick, would you go to a neighbor or to your Uncle Harry and ask them to operate on you? Of course you wouldn't.

If you need to make changes in your financial life, don't ask the opinion of people who have not been successful. Your brother-in-law or your neighbor Ralph will have lots of advice for you, but if they are not successful, the information will probably not be of much value.

It takes real courage to associate with successful people. It requires ambition and enthusiasm. Find successful people and do what they do.

 If you do what they do, you will have what they have. If you keep on doing what you are doing now, why should you expect to have a different lifestyle in five years?

Take courage from the wisdom of successful people. They are no different than you. They were simply fortunate enough to find a business system that could routinely produce successful results. They then took action to pay the price and let nothing stop them from reaching their dreams.

CHAPTER FIVE
THE PLIGHT OF THE
PROFESSIONAL

"On average, a doctor has his first heart attack at age 54." So says Florida physician Richard Fibleman.

Now I know what you're saying, you're not the average doctor. But if you are a professional, the stress of making a living may kill you!

Professionals are not exempt from the pitfalls that occur in the Corporate Kingdom. And professionals may be very susceptible to government harassment. (I mean regulation.)

Physicians

Consider the stress of a physician. Here is a person who went to four years of college, followed by four years of medical school, internship and residency. Then, if she or he wishes to specialize, they must obtain a fellowship and prepare for another three to four years.

Many doctors are well into their thirties before they start to earn a good salary.

While in their residencies and internships, they spend brutal hours making rounds and working in the emergency room. They are subjected to the whims and personalities of teaching physicians. It is not uncommon to have an intern work thirty hours in a row.

When they graduate, they have enormous educational debts - averaging $50,000, according to *Newsweek,* 4/93. And it is not unusual for a physician to spend in excess of $100,000 per year in malpractice insurance.

Of course there is the money. But what price does the physician pay for the privilege of earning a large income? In the United States, the average salary for a physician is $170,000. However, this includes the salaries for specialists and surgeons. In their article "Physicians Under The Knife," *Newsweek* editors estimate that general practitioners are much closer to $111,000 per year. This is not that much compared to the number of hours that a doctor works per week.

Their Spouse's Lifestyle

A former pediatric neurologist in Florida summed it up best. He said that most doctors create a lifestyle for their families, not for themselves. He tells of the time he returned home from work, late at night, and was almost bitten by the family dog. It seems that the dog did not recognize him!

Yes, doctors do own nice cars, fancy homes and country club memberships. They also drive their cars to work early in the morning, seldom see their homes in daylight and get "beeped" away from the table when dining at the country club.

The problems may be even greater for the physician who is in partnership with others. He or she must constantly worry about the malpractice liability of the rest of the group. And if a doctor gets sick, who takes care of him? His patients still require attention. His partners must fill in.

Other Professionals

Attorneys, engineers, architects and other professionals all suffer from the same problems in varying degrees. Each must put in long hours to compete.   This competition exists both within the firm and outside.

A young attorney is expected to put in 60 or more hours per week in order to attract the respect of the partners. And even when partnership is attained, he/she must continue to produce. The profits of the firm are usually divided according to the number of billable hours that a professional is able to generate.

Of course, there is an opportunity for professionals to build equity in a partnership. Some of them are able to retire with a sizeable residual income. However, this is only after many years of brutal work loads and tremendous stress. Still, it is better than working for a corporation and having no residual income upon retirement.

What Do Professionals Want?

For many professionals, especially doctors, more money will not solve the problems in their lives. In the research for this book, I have listened to many doctors talk about their disappointments in their professional lives. It is not the type of work they do that upsets them, it is the government red tape and the constant pressure to perform.

In the previously mentioned *Newsweek* article, 40% of the doctors surveyed reported that they would not go into the profession if they had it to do over again. Incredibly, nearly 40% of medical school applicants claimed that a physician tried to talk them out of the profession!

Attorneys and professionals involved in partnerships have the same complaints. They are responsible for billable hours. Each conversation, each bit of filing, becomes a task that must be billed out to a client.

These people are experiencing losses. They are losing time each day.

For the doctor, time is a precious commodity. Look at their waiting rooms. People are processed through as quickly as possible. There is a nursing staff, file clerks, billing clerks and insurance costs. To pay these monthly bills, the physician must see more and more patients.

What most physicians want is more time. Time to enjoy their families. Time to spend money. Time to practice the type of medicine that most of them entered the field for in the first place.

But under the current system, time is their enemy. Time means that the beeper will go off, that more patients must be seen and that the doctor will approach the age when it is no longer physically possible to maintain that heavy schedule.

The Professional's Scarcest Resource

If an attorney wishes to make more money, he/she can do one of two things. First, bill more hours. This is fine, except that there are only so many hours in the day. To increase effectiveness, associates can be hired to do some of the work. This will help to increase revenues, but it puts even more pressure on the attorney's time. Associates need to be supervised. Clients want to meet with the attorney, not the associates. Time runs out.

The alternative is to simply charge more per hour. This is fine to a certain extent. At some point, the fees are more than the attorney's service is worth. Competition precludes higher billing.

The scarcest resource for most professionals is time. An advertising agency manager once said that his entire inventory went home at night. That is, he sold the brain power of his staff. A professional does the same thing.

A professional spends years in school and apprenticeship to obtain a certification. Then, he must sell that knowledge and training to the highest bidder. Unfortunately, the professional cannot duplicate that knowledge in others unless they go through the same training and education.

So the only time that the professional can sell or trade for money is his time. And he only has so much of that.

Actually, anyone who works for a partnership or corporation is trading time for money. That is what a salary is. Professionals and partners trade time for capital or ownership. This is a better system, but it still has its limits. Usually the amount of time you have to trade is far greater than the rewards.

Duplication: The Secret To Success

People become professionals for a variety of reasons. There is prestige, money, lifestyle, etc. But what if there was a way for professionals to attain these things without all the stress and uncertainty that they now endure? Would that interest many professionals? You bet!

The answer is to find a system that can be duplicated. Where each member of the team has the same ability and incentive to generate income. Where there isn't just one "player" and a host of assistants. A system in which each person can equally share the responsibility and the rewards.

Ideally, these rewards would include time, independence, status, wealth, and an enjoyable lifestyle.

By duplicating themselves, a new breed of business professionals have put this theory into action. These people have created a system that is easy to use and produces fantastic results when diligent effort is applied.

The neurologist mentioned earlier in this chapter is one of the great examples of success through duplication. He was shown a system by a man who owned a surf shop.

Imagine, a surfer showing a system to a neurologist. But what the surfer and the doctor had in common was a system that allowed them to duplicate their time.

The reward for some people is money. For others, it is time. Still others enjoy the prestige that business success brings.

There is an old saying, "Give a man a fish, and he will have one meal. Teach him to fish and he will feed his family for life". This is the essence of duplication. Teach someone a simple system of duplication and income producing ideas. Then, participate in the rewards. You receive income not only from your own work, but from the work of others. And everyone has an equal opportunity to produce, regardless of education, certification or previous experience.

J. Paul Getty said "I would rather have one percent of the effort of 100 men than 100% of the effort of one man". He understood duplication.

If a professional cannot duplicate his/her work, and most can't, they are limiting themselves to 100% of the effort of one man.

So, What Do They Do?

There are three steps necessary for a professional or anyone else, for that matter, to take in order to break the cycle.

First: recognize the trap of trading time for dollars in a non duplicating profession.

Second: find a self-employed business and system that will help create a duplicating work force and can make money.

Third: put the same kind of effort into a system that you used to attain the degrees and training for the profession or occupation you serve.

This book is about a system. It may not be the answer to every professional's predicament, but it has worked for hundreds of thousands of people.

Systems require work. However, the work then produces both time and money. The time is yours to enjoy. The money is in the form of residual income.

The objective most working people look for - economic relief and the time to enjoy it.

Part Two:
What Have They Found?

CHAPTER SIX
PROFIT SHARING - WHY IT WORKS

What motivates people to work? For most of us, it is the simple fact that if we did not work, we would starve. Actually, in the United States, that is not exactly true. And this raises some interesting questions about why we work and how we can work better.

Survival vs. Self Esteem

Many people are familiar with Maslow's hierarchy of needs. Maslow determined that we fill our most basic needs first, then look for higher level rewards.

For example, we are not really concerned about status until we have made enough money to feed our families and provide the other basics of food and shelter. Once we have attained the basics, we are interested in things such as respect, and self esteem.

Most Americans know that if they lost their jobs, they would still have enough to eat. It may come from welfare payments, food stamps or a charity line, but we can all depend on the government for the most basic needs. We have a safety net.

So, why don't most Americans simply stop working and let the government feed and clothe us? Because MOST people have pride and self respect. And, to preserve our pride and our self esteem, we need to lead productive lives.

When I was doing the research for this book, I read many articles in magazines such as *Newsweek, Fortune, Forbes, The Wall Street Journal, U.S. News and World Report,* etc. that described people who had been laid off in the recession. Probably the most poignant was an article in *Parade Magazine,* 8/29/93, entitled "When Jobs Are Lost". It told the stories of eight people who had lost their jobs, and their struggle to find new employment.

Each of the people in this article described the financial hardships that the job loss created. But more importantly, all eight of the newly unemployed described the indignity of the situation. They felt devastated by their loss of esteem. This struck me deeply.

We work to create a proud, dependable and fulfilling life style; not simply to support our families at a subsistence level.

Free Enterprise

In a free enterprise system, we are all mini companies. We should use our talents to create wealth. If we work for someone else, we are creating wealth for them. If we work for ourselves, or if we participate in profit sharing, we create wealth for ourselves.

The portion we receive should be directly proportional to the contribution we made.

This is what separates free enterprise and capitalism from communism. In a communist state, everyone receives the same pay and benefits, no matter how hard they work. This is why communism will never survive. Why should people work hard when no matter what they do, they will have the same respect and lifestyle as everyone else? And, of course, we know what that lifestyle was like. Shoddy workmanship, shortages of goods, crumbling roads, etc. Yes, everyone had the same living style, but it was a terrible living style.

Unfortunately, our free enterprise system has begun to crumble as well. We are trading our enterprise for security, and the security has a price. We can never make the money we need to steadily improve our lifestyle. A wage slave in a good paying job is still a slave.

In a true free enterprise system, we should be able to make as much money as our dreams, ambitions and talents allow. There should be no ceiling on earnings.

Profit Sharing

In recent years, many companies have instituted what they call profit sharing. Under this system, employees are given compensation, usually shares of stock, that enable them to share in the profits of a company. In theory, the stock is given in proportion to the value of the employee's contribution. In actuality, the profit sharing is most often given in proportion to the employee's earnings. In fact, this is controlled by federal compensation laws. This is especially true when the profit sharing is granted through an employee retirement package that defers taxes.

Recently, however, the Corporate Kingdom has found ways to reward the kings and queens with a higher proportion of tax deferred profit sharing. An article in _National Underwriter_, 5/93, provides the details for putting more money into the pockets of the top executives.

 If top executives are interested in maximizing their profit sharing, we can assume that it is a good idea to participate in profit sharing yourself!

In other words, if the kings and queens want it, it must be a good thing to have.

Unfortunately, most of us will never have it. At least not in the manner we deserve.

The Original Concept

Gene Romagna, a partner in the consulting and training firm MARTA, located in Orlando Florida, is a major cheerleader for profit sharing. He understands how motivating it is to "reap what you sow". Gene asserts that many early American businesses did have profit sharing plans.

The early whaling and fishing industries were profit sharers. At the end of the voyage, each member of the crew received a share of the profits. The captain or owner would subtract the expenses of the voyage and distribute the remainder among the crew.

What did this do for the crew's motivation? For one thing, no one said "That's not my job". Everyone pitched in. If their crew worked together and produced a large catch, each man could expect better pay.

Apparently, there were no union bosses who would tell the captain "Don't ask that man to pull on the net, he is a fish scaler. If he has to pull on the net, we will all walk off the job".(Of course, if you walked off the job too far while aboard a whaling ship, you really had problems.)

Today, in the words of Romagna, "The profit sharing whaling ships and other companies have mostly gone to sea and drowned".

And this is a shame, because many people would work harder and achieve more - both personally and for their companies - if they could be rewarded with a share of the profits.

The Corporate Kingdom's Fear

We have already discussed how the Corporate Kingdom is afraid that their employees will make too much money. Yet, these fears are groundless.

There should be no ceiling on the amount that each employee can make.

If the company is making money, why should it matter how much an employee makes?

The reason the corporate kings will not allow employees to make unlimited incomes, is that the corporation always wants to pay you the least amount that it would take to replace you.

There is always someone who is willing to take your job. They may not do it as well, but if there are salary caps, no one is doing their job as well as they really could. So, the corporation can make more money by hiring someone at a lower rate of pay.

 But, if they simply linked your pay to your performance, you would make a lot more money - and so would they.

"The Employee Ownership 1000"

Of course, profit sharing is great. The only problem is when you stop contributing to profits, you can no longer share in them. Employee ownership is a long term, highly motivating practice that can make a huge difference in your retirement income.

 If you OWN part of a company, you continue to reap the benefits of profits even after you stop working. If you are sick or disabled, the work that you have already done will continue to contribute to your financial security.

Of course, ownership has a price. You may have to give up some rewards right now to build equity. For most of us, that would be fine, if in the end, we have residual income that continues to produce a paycheck even after we have stopped producing for the company.

There have been a number of companies that have developed employee ownership plans, according to the authors of _The New Owners_. They documented many companies that have employee ownership plans, usually through stock options. Unfortunately, the plans, in most cases, only _appear_ to provide real ownership. The authors identified the firms that had the largest ownership plans and listed them in their "Employee Ownership 1000".

According to Dr. Donald Schon, an MIT professor who reviewed _The New Owners_, only 5% of the companies in the "Employee Ownership 1000" practiced a realistic form of this motivational system. In addition, a mere one half of one percent were truly owned and operated by the employees.

What is your situation? Will you have residual income when you stop working? Can you stop working when you want? Or will you work the 40/50 plan and live on Social Security? The choice is yours, but you must make it now!

The New Breed

So, here are the facts, your company may have profit sharing, but it will not produce residual income. Your company may offer employee stock options, but this will not give you a chance to directly influence the company's performance or direction. You may even own your own business, but you are still limited by the amount of time that you can put into the business. And, the economy is in trouble and you want security for your family. What do you do?

Consider not investing thousands of dollars and weighing yourself down with employees, buildings, inventory and tons of paperwork. You should investigate the possibilities offered in Network Marketing.

After 20 years of business ownership, business education and teaching, and after two years of careful analysis in this particular field, I am making an independent and ernest recommendation that a few years ago I would have considered bold.

You should investigate the possibilities offered in Network Marketing.

The reason such a statement cannot be considered bold any longer is that network marketing companies, since the mid 1980's, have entrenched themselves with significant market shares and have continued to greatly out-perform their traditional competitors.

This system, sometimes called multilevel marketing(MLM), can provide an income stream that continues to grow even as direct involvement decreases. Multilevel marketing takes advantage of the power of duplication to make money and create a good lifestyle.

The full details on network marketing will be discussed in the next few chapters. For now, let's concentrate on the reasons people like you are increasingly moving to this opportunity.

The Direct Selling Association(DSA) has members such as Amway, Mary Kay Cosmetics, Nu Skin, etc. They recently conducted a survey to determine why people became involved with these companies. I should point out that direct selling and network marketing are not identical. However, most multilevel marketing companies are members of DSA, and the responses to the survey are likely to be similar for both groups.

Respondents of the survey were asked to rank their reasons for creating a business of their own. Consider these results: 87.5% said their liking for, and belief in the product were very important, 61% ranked supplemental income as very important, 51% were very attracted by the concept that working harder means making more money.

Also according to the DSA survey, participants saw the following *opportunities* in the business:

- Personal and professional growth
- Being your own boss
- Anyone can be successful
- Flexible schedules

The new breed of entrepreneur has limited their risk by limiting their investment and eliminating overhead. Yet, they can take advantage of the full benefits of duplicating their efforts.

In a multilevel marketing company, your work is duplicated by those in your "down-line". If you put in eight hours per week, and have six distributors in your line working eight hours, who each have four people in their lines working eight hours, there is a total of 248 hours of work in your organization.

 You profit from 248 hours of work, yet you have only worked eight. That's duplication, and that's power!

Your <u>8</u> hours
plus
6 distributors working 8 hours = <u>48</u>
plus
24 distributors (6 times 4) working 8 hours = <u>192</u>
equals
Total = 248 hours of work

The new breed of entrepreneurs have discovered an ethical, legal and simple way to make money and buy back their time. MLM is a system that has been around for almost 40 years, but is just now beginning to realize its full potential.

Are you courageous enough to face the facts and make a change in your life? If so, read the rest of this book as if your financial life depended on it. You know, it probably does!

CHAPTER SEVEN
MODERN MARKETING
THREE P's AND A D

Network marketing or multilevel marketing is not a brand new development. It really gained its fame when the Nutralite Vitamin Company (now owned by the Amway Corporation), implemented the concept in the 1950's. Today there are hundreds of companies that utilize a multilevel approach. Some of the biggest names in consumer goods and services utilize this approach for distributing their products.

Perhaps the most familiar examples are the long distance phone companies. Both Sprint and MCI have embraced a multilevel marketing system. MCI, for example, has created the "Friends and Family" program. MCI users sign up their most frequently called acquaintances and receive a discount. And that's all multilevel marketing is, consumers using and merchandising any goods or service and telling another consumer how to do the same, thus developing a network. It's that simple.

Using multilevel marketing and other techniques, MCI and Sprint captured 15% of the long distance market from AT&T. That's a sizeable percentage considering the monopoly originally granted to "MA BELL" had insured that they would have 100% of the business for years.

Of course, AT&T struck back with MLM plans of their own. Subscribers receive discounts for frequently called numbers. Of course, the numbers that you call must also utilize AT&T's service. So, consumers ask their friends and families, business contacts, etc. to use the same service. Everyone profits - especially the phone company.

MCI has taken the process one step further. They have joined forces with Amway, the oldest and largest MLM company. Amway distributors can actually MAKE money, not just save it, by creating a network of MCI users.

And this is the premise of multilevel marketing - create a network of consumers/merchants who use and merchandise the product and tell others how to do the same, then profit share, residually and long term, in direct proportion to the volume created.

But to understand MLM, it is first necessary to understand the overall marketing concept. In this chapter, we will discuss the *evolution* and *revolution* of the modern marketing concept.

Marketing Trends

The principles of marketing are based on one assumption - anything can happen! That's right, anything.

Having a good product is not enough. It must be placed into the hands of the consumer. And there is really no easy way of determining how the consumer will react to a product or its advertising. Marketing is unlike physics or chemistry. In the sciences, a certain amount of chemical A, combined with so many grams of chemical

B, will produce a reaction - an explosion perhaps. It will happen each time. But in marketing, the reaction is unknown.

Who could have foreseen the popularity of the Mini Van, the Pet Rock or the Slinky? Or, as Paul Zane Pilzer points out in *Unlimited Wealth*, Americans today eat 50% of their meals in restaurants. In 1960, they only ate 5% of their meals outside the home.

Recently, I was asked by a friend to explain why he should look at the MLM system. He had been introduced to the concept in the 1970's and had not reviewed it since. He was convinced that MLM was still door-to-door selling. I asked him three questions,

"In the 1970's, did you ever imagine that...

1) You would walk up to the wall outside your bank and get money out of a machine?

2) That your mother or your spouse would learn to pump their own gas at a gas station?

3) That you and your wife would have to both work full time just to afford a three bedroom house?"

Modern marketing has responded to new technologies and consumer demands.

Multilevel marketing is not a new idea, but it has changed to meet the needs of our times. It will continue to grow and change because it is based on people skills - not product skills.

The Marketing Variables

Marketers agree that there are two types of marketing variables - controllable and uncontrollable. It is the marketer's job to identify the uncontrollable variables and to create a product and promotion plan to work within them. The marketer also has the task of adjusting the controllable variables to make them fit into the world's realities.

That might sound confusing at first. But let's discuss the types of marketing variables and see how they fit into the MLM program.

Controllable Variables

Until recently, controllable variables were called the "Four P's of Marketing," or Product, Price, Promotion and Place. Products are goods and services. Price is the amount charged for a product. Promotion is the mixture of advertising and personal selling. Place is the retail store at which the products are sold.

Today, the overwhelming emphasis has shifted so greatly from *place* to *distribution*, that many marketers no longer discuss the four P's of marketing. Instead, they emphasize the "Three P's and a D".

Distribution has replaced place! Smart marketers no longer need retail outlets to put goods and services into the hands of the consumer.

Manufacturers like NIKE shoes and Firestone Tires, as well as service providers like Walt Disney, Hyatt Hotels and MCI are utilizing the power of MLM companies to distribute their products.

 Distribution will be the key to success in the 90's and beyond.

Uncontrollable Variables

Uncontrollable variables include the following:

- Economic
- Technological
- Political/Legal
- Sociological
- Competitive

The marketer has very little control over these variables. Yet, they have a great influence over the way in which goods and services are sold and distributed. So, the marketer must use the controllable variables to respond to the uncontrollable variables. Perhaps an example will help.

I have already mentioned the growth in the number of meals that Americans eat in restaurants. What created that demand? Changes in the uncontrollable variables created opportunities for marketers to utilize their controllable variables. Here's how:

In response to declining living standards (economic variable), more and more women began to enter the workforce. This created two factors. First, there was less time for these women to prepare dinner at home (sociological). Second, families had more disposable income (economic). Companies began to create restaurant concepts that were able to serve a limited menu quickly (competitive) and Congress enacted legislation to control franchising (political/legal). Communications equipment, computerized cash registers and microwave ovens (technological) made the consumers more conscious of speed and efficiency. They began to expect even faster service.

The restaurateurs used controllable variables to respond to the demand. They created the fast food concept (product) that focused on a few, easy to prepare items. They offered less service, but at a lower price (price). They knew that if they could capture the attention of children, they could get the rest of the family now and create a loyal, lifetime clientele. So, they advertised to the youngsters (promotion). Finally, they made the food available in as many locations as possible (place) and even created drive through windows and satellite locations in malls and schools (distribution).

While this is, admittedly, oversimplified, it does demonstrate the use of controllable and uncontrollable variables.

Uncontrollable Variables And MLM

Let's look at how uncontrollable variables affect **MLM** companies. We will see how many opportunities have been created and how needs are filled through network marketing.

Economic

Much of this book has been dedicated to exposing the inequities of the economic system that has been created by the Corporate Kingdom. People are _looking_ for answers to their economic conditions. MLM can provide that resource.

In addition, most MLM companies offer profit sharing and ownership to individuals. The MLM concept connects effort to rewards.

MLM offers new companies an opportunity to distribute their products without some of the massive start up costs. This enables more products to reach the marketplace.

Success Magazine, 5/92 discusses the phenomenal rise of the Nu Skin company. Founder and CEO Blake Rooney was able to build his company's sales to $500 million in 1991, without a paid, national sales force. According to _Success_, this allowed him to spend more money on product development and profit sharing.

Technological

Technological changes have created vast opportunities for wealth through MLM. An entrepreneur can get started with just a phone. Then, with a home office, computer, modem and fax machine, huge networks can be managed efficiently. Of course, there will never be a substitute for face to face contact, right? As James Bond would put it,"Never say never!"

Who would have predicted the huge boom in computer, television and catalogue sales? And the most amazing innovations are yet to come. A recent article in the venerable *Wall Street Journal,* discusses the advent of interactive television purchasing!

Political/Legal

In the U.S., MLM companies are controlled and regulated on both a national and state level. In fact, MLM companies are often held to a higher standard than other companies.

Unfortunately, there are unscrupulous members of any profession or industry and MLM has had its share. On the other hand, so has real estate, medicine, law and, of course, politics. When the stock market scandals of the 1980's occurred, people did not stop investing their money. While Ivan Boskey and his cronies spent time in jail for insider trading and fraud, the investors continued to place their money on Wall Street. MLM companies have suffered from an unfair backlash, but the good ones are still thriving.

According to *New Business Opportunities Magazine*, (10/92) the Federal Trade Commission charged that the Amway company, "one of MLM's biggest and most respected companies" was an illegal pyramid. On May 8, 1978 they were cleared after four years of legal battle.

"If Amway hadn't withstood the FTC's challenge, there would be no MLM industry today" said Jeff Babener of Babener & Associates, an Oregon based firm specializing in direct merchandising issues.

MLM companies are regulated by the FTC under Article five which prohibits unfair trade practices. Companies that make exaggerated claims or operate as an illegal pyramid can be prosecuted. This regulation has helped to insure that reputable MLM companies will not be injured by the few bad operators who seem to show up in every industry.

Of course, legal and political activity also affect potential distributors. Many physicians have chosen MLM to provide stability against uncertain times. The changes in health care legislation make practicing medicine a very stressful business.

Sociological

The economical changes that have driven 63% of married women into the work force have created sweeping sociological changes. We are now a more mobile society. Families are almost as likely to move to fit the woman's career as the man's. The traditional extended family is certainly less visible, and grandparents are no longer on hand to help with raising the family. People have less time to shop.

Enter MLM. With networking, products come more directly to the consumer. *Forbes Magazine*, 5/93 provides ample information about the changing sociological trends and their affect on business. According to *Forbes*, Americans are spending less time in the mall and visiting fewer stores per trip. In addition, they are ordering almost twice as many goods and services from catalogues.

Changing sociological customs present many opportunities. Single women have learned to be capable managers of both home and the workplace. They are now entering the MLM field and achieving success. They utilize their time better and have higher aspirations than a generation ago.

Competitive

Competition has two sides to it. First, the number of firms in the MLM business is growing. Yet markets for consumer/merchant distributors are far from saturated. And, consumer/merchant distributors tend to be very loyal to their own products.

 Success Magazine, 3/92 reports that people's loyalty is switching from stores to specific brands. This heavily favors a distributor with a reliable product.

The other competitive factor inherent in MLM is that people work together as teams. Success is built on the success of others. This has been a powerful concept. It reduces competition between people and encourages them to work together, in a network. The new phase of competition was predicted in John Naisbitt's powerhouse book *Megatrends*.

Controllable Variables And Multilevel Marketing

MLM is a serious form of marketing. As such, the MLM distributor is on the front line of the marketing company.   The   sections   below   discuss   the implementation of MLM through the four controllable marketing variables. The discussion is brief, because the next three chapters provide greater insight into these functions.

Product

The basis for any MLM program is to have a truly superlative product. It should be guaranteed and backed with the full weight of the company.

Some MLM companies, such as Amway, carry their own products, as well as the lines of other firms. In the case of Amway, over 450 of the Fortune 500 companies distribute their products through the Amway Network. Other network marketing ventures move their own products exclusively. Nu Skin, Matol and Mary Kay Cosmetics are three giants that operate in this manner.

Price

Prices must be competitive or the buyers will simply shop elsewhere. Wal-Mart built its entire reputation on a low price concept. Of course, in traditional retailing, a low price means less service. That cannot be the case for MLM companies. While their prices need to be competitive, their service is usually beyond the customer's expectations.

MLM is far removed from a wholesale buying club. It's incentive is not in creating a savings plan, but rather, in creating an income stream that continues to increase with time. Shopping smartly at discount houses has little power compared to creating a profit sharing pool of consumer/merchandising habits.

Competitive prices do not necessarily imply that all MLM's should sell their products at heavy discounts. Price is a combination of product quality, service level, and convenience.

Promotion

Promotions range from advertising to public relations to direct selling. All of these are considered parts of the promotion variable.

A good MLM company supports its salesforce with training, high quality brochures and samples, and advertising.

The best companies provide their consumer/merchants with a "packaged" system. It contains support material for both retailing and attracting new consumer/merchants.

Distribution

 MLM IS distribution. It is the process of putting products and services into the hands of the consumers.

The best MLM companies will have the following features for their consumers/merchants:

- ample inventory available
- fast delivery
- free pick up for returned items
- an easy ordering system
- money back guarantee

A Final Word

Merchandising is not an exact science. But the great MLM companies have helped to take some of the mystery and uncertainty out of the process. Their systems are worthy of your investigation. Many thousands have found financial security and freedom by using this fast evolving economic movement.

If you are of the entrepreneurial spirit, you would do well to gain a deeper understanding of the system that, given the past seven year growth rate, will probably create the largest form of merchandising the world will see.

CHAPTER EIGHT
WHAT THE EXPERTS SAY

Close your eyes and imagine the following:

Time Warner Inc. has just announced the creation of an interactive cable channel called the *Full Service Network*. The channel will allow viewers to enter an electronic "mall" through their television sets. Once inside the mall, viewers can enter and browse in individual stores that carry name brands.

Spiegel Catalog has agreed to be one of the first shops. They will feature their *Eddie Bauer* line in the store. Other catalog companies and retailers are expected to sign on with the service. Soon, shoppers will be able to shop at any time, day or night, even on holidays. They will pay for the merchandise by credit card and have it shipped to their homes.

Imagine how convenient this will be! No long lines. No screaming children - yours or anyone else's! No braving the cold, the damp, or the heat.

Does this sound like a dream? It shouldn't. Interactive shopping networks are already on-line. The future is here now.

Presently, catalog shopping is a 51 billion dollar industry. And as Spiegel president Jack Shea said in the *Orlando Sentinel*, this will offer his company increased channels of distribution.

Where will you be when network marketing goes "network"? Do you have the vision and determination to grab your piece of the future? Or, will you still be listening to some of your friends, ignoring the wave of opportunities that will carry hundreds of thousands into unlimited opportunity?

I just don't know how to say it to you more strongly. Don't miss this opportunity!

The Fall Of The Mall

One of my favorite articles about the changes in personal buying habits is "The Fall Of The Mall", *Forbes Magazine*, 5/93. This article chronicles the slow decline of traditional shopping methods.

There has been a drop off in visits to the mall, number of shops visited and expenditures per visit. But there has not been a fall in purchases! People are still buying, they are just doing it differently.

And network marketing is their alternative!

In 1991, consumers purchased $42 BILLION worth of goods and services by check or credit card from their homes! That is an increase of 30% from 1988.

At the same time, sales in retail stores declined by 3%. SO, more is being purchased each year - and it is coming from non-traditional sources.

The number of people shopping by catalog has doubled in the last decade. Last year, 102 million people made at least one purchase from a catalog.

The Growth Of MLM's

While the malls decline, MLM's are growing like crazy.

 In Success Magazine, 3/92, the futurist Faith Popcorn declared "in the 90's, instead of going to the store, the store will come to us."

Consumers are buying much more than a product. They are purchasing information, service, and convenience.

So what is the logical next step? To create a store that enters your home, with information about products, and a convenient delivery system. That is progress and it is what consumers want.

 The Wall Street Journal estimates that by the end of the decade, over 50% of all goods and services will be available through MLM companies.

I am skeptical when I read some sources, but the *Wall Street Journal* has never been known to jump to conclusions!

In *Success Magazine*, 5/93, author Nichol Woolsey Biggart of the University of Chicago says, "Nothing in recent history has grown as fast as direct selling organizations such as Amway, Nu Skin and Mary Kay Cosmetics."

They are right.   And it is because both new and established businesses are joining the MLM family.

 In the Ocala Star Banner, internationally syndicated business columnist Allan Fishman estimates that the total sales from MLM companies exceeds $100 billion per year, and that there are over seven million people who are actively involved as distributors around the world.

These people are only involved for one reason - they want to change their lives by increasing their incomes.

The Revolution Is Technological

Would you deny the computer revolution?   It has happened. People HAVE adapted to technology. They HAVE changed their buying habits.

Paul Zane Pilzer, in *Success Magazine*, says that

Wealth = Physical Resources X Technology

That is, we can increase our wealth by changing our technology, regardless of our physical resources. So, if your time is limited, use technology to increase your wealth.   If you are not as smart as your neighbor, use technology to increase your wealth. If you are not tall, athletic, handsome, educated, etc., simply use the technology of the day to improve your wealth.

> *Technology does not refer to computers! It is not fancy machinery! It is something that is available to everyone!*

Technology is simply knowledge. If you have read this book to this point, you already have the knowledge you need to make money to become totally financially free.

In this case, the technology is networking. In the next chapter, we will look at the things you need to be successful in a network. And they are simple: commitment, energy, enthusiasm, etc.

These attributes are all you need to put the technology of networking to work for you.

They Saw The Light

Network marketing has been called the "People's Franchise" by Burke Hedges in *Who Stole The American Dream*. He is right. It was first discovered by ordinary people. People who wanted to change their lives, make more money, achieve their dreams.

And at first, they were alone. Not any more.

Four hundred and fifty of the Fortune 500 companies distribute their products through the MLM system. And many direct selling companies have made the switch.

According to Hedges, Fuller Brush and Avon are only two of the recent additions. They discovered the power of this concept. MCI and Sprint were leaders in telecommunications that utilize MLM's. AT&T soon followed.

Success Magazine, 3/92 reports that the following companies have started, or are planning to start, distributing through MLM companies:

> Colgate/Palmolive
> Gillete
> Campbell's Soup
> General Foods

In fact, there is virtually no product or service that cannot be moved through MLM. The only remaining barriers are for fresh foods, which may become spoiled. But even this is changing. Amway offers a gift package that contains gourmet meats.

Get ready, because MLM will soon dominate the food chain!

Is There Hope For The "Little Guy" ?

With all of these big names in the MLM business, you may have two concerns. First, can the little guy make it? Second, is the market for MLM companies becoming saturated? The answers are "Absolutely" to the first question and "No Way!" to the second.

The little guy is the backbone of the MLM. It is the single person, couple or small group that starts the network. Scott (not his real name) was a little guy. He was an auto mechanic, and his wife was a secretary. They had nothing, yet have become financially set through MLM. He left a message on an associate's voice mail this past week. He was in Scotland, working on his network. But he had taken the day off. He called from St. Andrews golf course where he had just finished a round of golf with some MLM friends. Way to go, Scott!

In my research for this book, I came in contact with many people like Scott. Some were doctors, others were real estate agents, football players or businessmen. Their common link is wealth. They obtained that wealth by taking the first step. They shared their business with others, helped them grow and reaped huge rewards.

Of course, there is another reason why MLM companies will always be for the little guy. Even though Fortune 500 companies are involved in MLM's, they are not distributors. The large companies only want to send their products through the MLM lines. It is still the individual consumer that is the KING.

YOU are the most important part of the MLM system. YOU will be rewarded for your effort.

MLM is big business - for the little guy.

Saturation - Never!

Paul Pilzer explains the basic premise for continued growth in consumption in "Economic Paradigms," a tape produced by _Internet_. According to his premise, people will always want something. It is the nature of the free enterprise system.

He uses the example of a recent college graduate who buys a new suit for $200. After two days on the job, he realizes that he needs another suit to wear. He spends another $200. Soon, he has ten suits.

If we accept the fears of saturation, we would assume that he would never buy another suit. But soon, he wants a nicer suit. So, he spends $500 on a new one. Now, the other suits don't seem so nice. So, he replaces the rest of the $200 suits with $500 suits.

Then, one day, he buys a suit for $1,000...

To assume that MLM markets will become saturated is to assume that no new products will be introduced. We know that will not happen.

Of course, some people say "Well soon, everyone will be in an MLM. There won't be anyone for me to teach. How can I build an organization?"

Is everyone you know in an MLM? Of course not. Some people will never get into one. They will cling to the hope that trading their time for dollars will someday make them wealthy - if they don't get laid off.

Right now, in the whole world, there are not enough people in network marketing to replace the population of New York City!

More people enter the workforce and graduate from high school each year. Are they already involved in network marketing? NO.

Have we run out of people to eat hamburgers, buy cars or new homes?

NO.

 If you are using the fear of saturation as an excuse to avoid making the commitment to your family's financial success, you are wrong. You'll have to find another excuse.

Will Your MLM Company Grow?

Once you have understood that MLM will benefit you, you must choose the correct company. Not all MLM companies are created equal. You have to carefully select a company that will grow and support you. *Success Magazine,* 1/93 warns that "85% of all MLM ventures fail within the first 18 months." This should not be surprising, as many new businesses will fail within that time. Yet, the company's age is not a guarantee of success.

In the same article, the author urges networkers to use "due diligence" when selecting their MLM company. He lists the following things to examine. It is great advice!

I have selected the six criteria that I think are the most important.

Evaluating Your MLM Opportunity

1.   Age of the company
    •   Generally, avoid start ups.

2.   Steady sales growth

3.   Financial package
    ● Compensation checks, start up costs, bonuses, etc. Very important - are there minimum purchases or monthly sales requirements? Are there non-performance penalties?

4.   Departmentalization
    ● Are there departments for distributor relations, accounting, etc?

5.   Products
    ● The major factor. Is it consumable, desirable, priced right, approved, etc.? The products or services are the real reason that the MLM concept can work.Is the product guaranteed? What are the buy back policies?

6.   The system
    ● The great MLM companies supply a complete system for success. This includes not only brochures, catalogs and advertising materials, but also training and support. Plug yourself into a good system and follow it. Look for a company that can provide you with the support you need.

Grow And Be Wealthy

There is no doubt that the MLM concept is growing fast. It will provide opportunities for anyone who wishes to participate with a good company. Of course, some opportunities will be better than others. Choose your MLM company carefully.

But, as the advertisement says,"JUST DO IT".

There are no excuses large enough to prevent you from taking advantage of this remarkable system. You should see some of the people who have already done it. They are not special. Most of them did not even own a business before in their lives. Yet, they have made money and changed their lives.

It is up to you. Do you have the power to do it? You do.

Can you do it? Yes you can!

Will you do it? Only you can make the choice. But if you choose not to do it, you will miss the greatest single opportunity that has ever been available for the ordinary person.

Don't say no to the "People's Franchise".

CHAPTER NINE
HOW MONEY IS MADE

It is through efficient distribution that MLM companies make the huge profits that are shared with the distributors. Think of it, MLM entrepreneurs are *called* distributors. They have created an alternative distribution system.

For a clear understanding of how money is made in MLM, read "The Golden Door To Wealth," in *Success Magazine*, 3/93.

According to the article, the cost of goods today in a retail store is 15% manufacturing costs and *85% distribution costs*. (This includes wholesalers, jobbers, sales representatives and retail costs.) This is almost exactly the opposite of what it used to be.

At the turn of the century, only 15% of the costs were from distribution. The remaining 85% were incurred during manufacture. So, in order to save money, the emphasis was placed on cutting the costs of the manufacturing process.

During the early days of this century, vast fortunes were made by inventors who simplified manufacturing. Eli Whitney's cotton gin is an excellent example. The Bessemer furnace improved steel production. Henry Ford introduced the assembly line, and made it affordable for almost everyone to own a car.

"Today, however, the great opportunities (for creating wealth) lie in distribution. In the past two decades, the majority of great personal fortunes have been made by people who found better ways of distributing things."(Success Magazine, 5/93)

New Alliances

The cost of inventory and distribution has created some amazing alliances among business. The Japanese initiated a cost saving system in the 1970's called "just in time" purchasing. Although it is applied mostly to manufacturing plants, it is the basis for "just in time" retailing, which is the backbone of MLM distribution.

Just in time purchasing was first implemented in American automobile manufacturing. Instead of carrying enough inventory for a month or a week, the automobile manufacturers began to limit their inventory needs to just a few hours.

This cut their cost of storage and inventory capital expenditures. This, in turn, cut the cost of their cars to consumers.

However, it became critical that their suppliers would be able to deliver the raw materials to them at a moment's notice. So, the suppliers began to build warehouses right next to the auto plants. The two facilities were connected by railroad tracks, and the suppliers bore the costs of inventory - not the auto manufacturer.

It was easier for the supplier to store the materials. After all, they were specialists in their particular line. They may have stored, sold and delivered only steel. On the other hand, under the old system, the auto manufacturer had to handle and store great quantities of steel, rubber, vinyl. etc.

The efficiency created by "just in time" purchasing saved money in the distribution system and made money for both the supplier and the manufacturer.

Wal-Mart: Just In Time

The Wall Street Journal, 12/91, filed a report on Wal-Mart's decision to shorten its incoming channels of distribution by eliminating independent sales reps. (Manufacturers hire independent sales reps when they cannot afford to hire their own sales staff. These reps receive a commission on what they sell, thereby adding to the cost of distribution.) Wal-Mart will only deal directly with manufacturers, through a sophisticated computer system.

Why should you care about Wal-Mart and their suppliers? Because the opportunity for a manufacturer to distribute through an MLM can produce the same benefits as using a huge merchandiser like Wal-Mart, without most of the disadvantages!

In other words, you are part of the world's best system of distribution - and you will share in the profits!

Who Benefits From MLM Distribution - And How?

There are four major beneficiaries from MLM distribution:

    1. The Manufacturer
    2. The MLM Company
    3. Distributors
    4. Consumers

The obvious benefit to the manufacturer is greater income - both through savings and increased sales. The manufacturer benefits from reduced costs, because the distributors are almost always independent contractors.

In some cases, like Nu Skin, the manufacturer and the MLM company are the same entity. Nu Skin distributors only move products that are produced by the Nu Skin company. However, Amway entrepreneurs represent not only the Amway household line, but also a line of over 5,000 different products and services from thousands of other manufacturers. The brands they distribute include such names as Kellog's, Sanyo, and Nike.

Distributors make money in two ways in most MLM companies. First, they can retail products, buying them at wholesale and selling them for retail. Second, MLM companies offer a bonus or override on the volume created in a group of sponsorship.

This means that large sums of money that would have been eaten by the distribution process are held by the MLM company. This money is given to distributors, based on the amount of volume they generate.

That's right, the money is just sitting there, waiting for some enterprising and industrious distributor to earn it.

The money is generally awarded on a sliding scale. A small volume might receive a 5% bonus from the MLM company. On the other hand, a distributor with large volumes of business could receive 25% in overrides from the MLM company. And there are generally no salary caps!

The final beneficiary is the consumer. The modern consumer is faced with a serious dilemma; how to get quality merchandise without wasting time at the mall and other outlets?

According to *Forbes Magazine*, 5/93, consumers are spending less time shopping in malls. They are no longer shopping for recreation. In 1982 shoppers spent an average of 90 minutes in the mall and visited an average of 3.6 stores. In 1992, they stayed only 78 minutes and visited 2.6 stores.

A Final Word On Distribution

Distributing goods and services through an MLM is the wave of the future and is profitable right now. In order to take advantage of the financial benefits, a distributor must identify a solid company that has a product people want. Consumables make the best choice, because they are used again and again.

So look over your opportunities and get started. You now have the knowledge to understand why MLM distribution works. Make it work for you!

CHAPTER TEN
A NETWORKING FRENZY

Money is made in networks. That's true and here is the great news - you are already in networks! That's right. Whether you want it or not, you are a networker.

Do you belong to any professional groups? How about service groups, such as the Lion's Club, Rotary, Loyal Order of the Whatever? Do you have a circle of friends? When you see a good movie, do you tell your friends?

These are all networks.

We belong to networks because we are human, and that is how we operate best. We work with others.

Networkers share their experiences. They help each other. They cooperate.

When you go to work, does your boss say to you, "Are you making all the money you need? Can we help you to reach your dreams? Is there something I can do to help you today?" Probably not, but your network might.

A network is a family of people, working together to help one another. Networkers do things for each other. They use their collective skills to solve each other's problems.

The Network Is The Thing

John Naisbitt, author of _Megatrends_ has predicted the rise of networks. He says that the usual corporate structure, a hierarchy with rigid ranks and levels, is not conducive to human achievement. It makes it too hard to get information.

In a hierarchy, people sit on information and keep it to themselves. Why? Because information is power and they don't want you to have power.

 But in a network, information is shared. And this means that everyone has power.

With power comes performance. And with performance comes rewards: money, growth, stability.

The modern network is not limited to a single corporation or program. For example, a real estate agent from one company might find other real estate agents, in other cities, who share professional information. This is a network.

The power to achieve your goals can come from sharing information.

Networks Are For Everyone

Networks are not exclusive. There is only one rule: if you can contribute, you can belong. That is the great equalizer - your ability to help others in the system.

We often hear about the "good old boy network". Forget it, it's dead. The network of the 90's and beyond will help people adapt to change - not fight it.

People no longer have time for inefficient hierarchies and road blocks to information.

A study reported in Megatrends indicates that it takes seven phone calls to get information from a government agency. In a network, members use "connections" to cut through red tape and get the job done.

Networks And MLM's

A network is a perfect structure for an MLM. It is the cooperation among individuals that produces results. MLM's depend on networks.

Finis Welch, a labor economist, reports in *Fortune Magazine*, 9/92, that "We are in the midst of a big league revolution, which is devaluing physical skills in favor of mental skills". A networker concentrates on the power of the mind. He/she looks ahead, sees problems and uses the help of others to overcome them.

In MLM, networkers have seen the future and it is troubling. So they band together and solve problems.

MLM companies not only distribute products and services through networks, they pass information as well.

For example, many MLM companies use information they receive *back* from their distributors to improve products and services. This is two way communication at its finest.

Networks, like politics, are local. Networks start with one person.   According to *Megatrends*, everyone is at the center of a network. In MLM, distributors have up-lines and down-lines to help them achieve their goals.

Imagine that! People working together! Well, it works - and it works BIG!

The Joy Of Networking

 Imagine yourself, succeeding in your most ambitious dreams, not by yourself, but in the company of people who really care about you.

Please read that sentence again.

It should hit you like a thunderclap. A network is a family. People who actually care about each other.

What would it mean to you to have some help? Real help! When was the last time someone did some of your work? Do you have some neighbors or family members that help you out - and that you help?

Now imagine an entire business of people helping each other. Wouldn't that be something?

In network marketing, people help each other to distribute products. And, they make money doing it. Lot's of money.

When you go to an MLM meeting, what is the first thing you notice? People are happy, not just for themselves, but for others. In network marketing, when someone succeeds, so does everyone else! This happens all the time.

Watch the distributors being called up on stage at conventions to receive pins, flowers, badges, etc. They are making money. Why is everyone else clapping? Because they're making money too. Now isn't that something?

What would it take for you to get involved with some other people who want you to make money? Do you think they are faking their enthusiasm? Think again.

 No one stays in a network unless they are getting something out of it. For some people it is recognition. For others, it is money. For still others, it is a sense of belonging. For most though, it is the MONEY - and all that it can bring.

To Build A Network...

Building a network is simple - if you have something worth giving. It has to be something special and valuable.

Now, read this carefully. You become successful in a network when you help other people reach their goals. Got it? Get it!

That's what it takes to build a successful network. Help others to succeed. If you are in the right business, you will profit from the success you build for others. Wow, will you profit!

You have something very special to share if you are in a network marketing business. You have opportunity. But opportunity is only part of the equation. The people in your network must take advantage of the opportunity by applying themselves. And to do this, they will need your help.

You will need the help of others. Your up-line will provide you with that help. It is your network at work.

Geometric Progression

How does a network work? Through geometric progression.

Suppose you start a network marketing business. You share the business with other people, offering them an opportunity. If they see the business as beneficial, they will join.

When they share the opportunity with other people, the business grows geometrically.

For example, if YOU show five people how to create their own business, and they each share the business with five others, there are now 31 people in the business.

YOU	= 1
Your next 5 distributors	= 5
They each sponsor 5 distributors(5 x 5)	= <u>25</u>
Total	= 31

That's a geometric progression. You benefit from the total volume created.

Suppose that you put in ten hours per week on the business. If each of the other people in your group work 10 hours per week, there are now 310 hours being spent, and you benefit from all of them! Meanwhile, you continue to put just ten hours of your own in.

Now don't get confused and think that you are making money *FROM* each of these distributors. Remember our chapter on distribution? You learned that through MLM's, tremendous quantities of money could be saved by shortening the distribution channel. Instead of spending money on salespeople, retail store overhead, etc., these savings are given to the distributors.

That is where the money comes from. The company sends you a bonus, based on the volume in your group.

Everyone is rewarded according to their effort and performance. Each person shares in the profits of the company, based on the volume that they cause to be generated.

Does that make sense to you? It should.

 It is free enterprise, rewarding the people who produce, without taking it out of the pockets of other people who are producing. And, there are absolutely no limits to the amount of money that can be made.

There are no bosses holding back information. There is no one to say "Wait a minute, this guy is making more than me."

In fact, your sponsor would be delighted if you made lots of money. He or she would actually be excited if you made more than they did.

You want the people in your group to be wealthy, very wealthy. If they are, you will be too. That's the beauty of networking. Help others to reach their goals. Yours will be in the bag!

So What Do You Need To Do?

This is the obvious question. At least I hope it is obvious by now. You need to do something and you need to do it right away.

Do it now!

Start by making a commitment. Make it to yourself, your family, and eventually, to your down-line. Find a network marketing company that fits your needs and stick with it.

Let me share with you the words of Alan Fishman, the syndicated business columnist:

> "Those who are successful in a multilevel business are generally those who are willing to make a six month or more commitment to developing their distribution system and have become tied in with a quality product or service. In most cases, the successful distributors handle products that are consumable and need to be replaced."

He has hit the nail on the head. Have a great product or service, especially one that is consumable, and share it with others, while making a strong COMMITMENT to the concept.

A Question Of Priorities

Why will you do this? Because your life has taken on new priorities. You are working hard now so that you will not have to later on. You are making choices now, so that later, you can make more exciting choices.

Don't get caught in the same ruts. Put a jump-start on your life. Consider the advice from "Charismatic Capitalism" in *Success Magazine*, 5/93. It states that most MLM companies encourage their distributors to serve "God first, family second, career third".

Keep this in mind. You need to help others to make their commitment to strong values and worthwhile goals.

It Will Happen!

Imagine a life spent with successful people, working together. You have a strong family, high personal values and you are making money.

You have worked in the free enterprise system, using honesty and your God given determination to accomplish some wonderful goals. Does that sound like a progressive, rewarding life?

It is the life that you were promised when you first discovered the blessings of liberty. It is the life you deserve.

 John Paul Getty, in his book, *How To Be Rich*, claims that there are six conditions for success in business. He should know.

Here they are:

- **Be in business for yourself**

- **Market a product or service that is in great demand**

- **Guarantee that product or service**

- **Give better service than the competition**

- **Reward those who do the work**

- **Build your success upon the success of others**

Multilevel marketing - network marketing is all of these things.

Use your God given talents, hold firmly on to your liberty, and grab the future.

The opportunity is available to anyone. It truly is becoming the Peoples' Franchise!

BIBLIOGRAPHY

Administrative Science Quarterly,"The New Owners: The Mass Emergence of Employee Ownership in Public Companies and What It Means to American Business," March 1993.

Advancing the American Dream, Direct Selling Association

Amagram,"The Future Is Now," January 1990.

The Atlanta Journal,"Who Will Hire Me Now?," August 29, 1993.

The Atlanta Journal,"A New Captain Takes the Helm at Amway," August 1, 1993.

Business Opportunity, July 1993.

Business Tokyo,"Amway Leads The Way," November 1989.

BusinessWeek,"Work & Family," June 28, 1993.

BusinessWeek,"The Information Revolution," Spring 1994.

BusinessWeek,"Retailing Will Never be the Same," July 26, 1993.

BusinessWeek,"Why Hit the Middle Class? That's Where the Money Is?," March 1, 1993.

BusinessWeek,"Executive Pay: Clinton's Curbs are Out of Touch - And Out of Bounds," March 22, 1993.

BusinessWeek,"What Happened to the American Dream?," August 19, 1991.

BusinessWeek,"Is Interactive TV So Much Hype?" May 11, 1993.

BusinessWeek,"Shopping By Cable And Phone," November 2, 1992.

BusinessWeek,"It's A Lot Tougher To Mind The Store," January 8, 1990.

Citrus County Chronicle,"Networks, Not Pyramids," February 21, 1993.

The Dentist,"Network Marketing: A Profitable Option," June 1992.

Department of Health & Human Services Publication,"Heart Attacks and Mondays," March 1991.

Don't Let Anybody Steal Your Dream, by Dexter R. Yager Sr., 1993.

Forbes,"The Death of the Salesman," May 24, 1993.

Forbes,"The 400 Largest Private Companies in the U.S.," December 7, 1992.

Forbes,"The Power Of Positive Inspiration," December 9, 1991.

Forbes,"Soap and Hope In Tokyo," September 3, 1990.

Fortune,"What's Happening To Jobs In America," July 12, 1993.

Fortune,"A Brave New Darwinian Workplace," January 25, 1993.

Fortune,"How To Protect Your Financial Future," January 25, 1993.

Fortune,"Are Strategic Alliances Working?" September 21, 1992.

Fortune,"Burned-Out Bosses," July 25, 1994.

Fortune,"Waking up to the New Economy," June 27, 1994.

Fortune,"The Truth About The Rich And The Poor," September 21, 1992.

<u>Goal Setting</u>, by Zig Ziglar, 1993.

Harpers Magazine,"Average CEO Earnings," September 1993.

<u>How to be Rich</u>, by J. Paul Getty.

Inbound Logistics,"A Revolution's A'Coming," April 1994.

122

Income Opportunities,"10 Top Network Marketing Companies," September 1993.

<u>Megatrends</u>, by John Naisbitt, 1982.

Nadler, Beverly, "Multi Level Marketing."

Nation's Business,"Selling American to the Japanese," October 1990.

National Underwriter,"Sweetening The Pot For Key Execs," May 3, 1993.

<u>Network & Multi-Level Marketing</u>, by Allen Carmichael, 1991.

New Business Opportunities,"Step Up to Success...As Multilevel Marketing Cleans Up Its Act," October 1992.

NEWSWEEK,"There's Still No Free Lunch," April 12, 1993.

NEWSWEEK,"Doctors Under The Knife," April 5, 1993.

Ocala Star Banner,"Be Your Own Boss With Only Hundreds of Dollars," November 28, 1991.

The Orlando Sentinel,"Magazine Flushes Out Tough Bosses," September 29, 1993.

The Orlando Sentinel,"Spiegel Unwraps Retail Channels," September 28, 1993.

The Orlando Sentinel, "Cutbacks Not Always Best Option," September 16, 1993.

The Orlando Sentinel, "Worker's Priorities Undergo Upheaval," September 15, 1993.

Pennsylvania Hospitals Nineties, "Futurist Predicts Collaboration Holds Promise for Healthier Future," August 2, 1993.

The Reporter, "Workers in Gridlock," September 6, 1993.

Review of Social Economy, "Smith's View on Human Nature: A Problem in the Interpretation," 1977.

Success, "Global Paradox," March 1994.

Success, "The Greatest Motivator," December 1993.

Success, "Unlimited Wealth," October 1993.

Success, "Unlimited Future," September 1993.

Success, "Charismatic Capitalism," May 1993.

Success, "The $4-Billion Man," May 1993.

Success, "The Mindset of the Rich," March 1993.

Success, "Look Before You Leap," January/ February 1993.

Success, "Magic Marketing," March 1992.

124

Success,"We Create Millionaires," March 1992.

Success,"The New Feudalism," January 1992.

Success,"Network Marketing," May 1990.

U.S. Department of Labor,"What Work Requires of Schools."

U.S. News & World Report,"White Collar Wasteland," June 28, 1993.

U.S. News & World Report,"On the Wrong Track," May 10, 1993.

Unlimited Wealth, by Paul Zane Pilzer

Upline,"Network Marketing and the American Dream," March 1993.

USA Today,"Many In 50s Face Hard Years," June 18-20, 1993.

The Wall Street Journal,"Hungarians Seeking To Find a New Way Find Instead Amway," January 15, 1993.

The Wall Street Journal,"Wal-Mart Set to Eliminate Reps, Brokers," December 2, 1991.

Who Stole The American Dream?, by Burke Hedges, 1992.

Your Next Move(Internet Services Corporation),"The Price Of Success," 1990.

Appendix A

Goal Setting

You can't hope to achieve your objectives unless you know what they are! This is your opportunity to clearly state your goals. But that is just the first step.

After you set your goals, you need a plan for reaching them. You will learn about a system that can help you reach them. That is the purpose of this book.

First, however, we would like you to clearly establish your future. Describe your goals in detail. Set a date for achieving them.

Goal Category	Description	Date
Vehicles		
Home		
Debt Free		
Education		
Retire		
Helping Others		
Church/Charity